£3.00

BIRDS OF THE WORLD
SEABIRDS

BIRDS OF THE WORLD
SEABIRDS

JOHN P.S. MACKENZIE

HARRAP
LONDON

Copyright © 1987 by Key Porter Books

First published in Great Britain 1987 by HARRAP Ltd.
19/23 Ludgate Hill, London EC4M 7PD

Originally published in Canada by Key Porter Books Limited, Toronto

ISBN: 0-245-54593-X

Design: First Image
Composition: First Image

Printed and bound in Hong Kong
Scanner Art Services, Toronto

87 88 89 90 6 5 4 3 2 1

Page 2: White Pelican (*Pelecanus erythrorhynchos*)   When fishing these
pelicans move forward in a line, driving their prey before them. They scoop
up fish while floating on the water.

Pages 4-5: The Ivory Gull (*Pagophila eburnea*)   This gull wanders through the
the Arctic in winter, and into the Atlantic as far south as Newfoundland in
summer. It sometimes follows Inuit hunters in search of scraps.

CONTENTS

Gentoo Penguin (*Pygoscelis papua*)   These large penguins come ashore to
nest between August and October. The young depart between December
and March, and the adults leave by June.

INTRODUCTION

Horned Grebe (*Podiceps auritus*)   This grebe nests in a wide band across the Northern Hemisphere, usually in small marshy ponds. In winter, most birds move to salt water.

Birds of the oceans are members of those species that take all, or almost all, of their livelihood from the sea. Typically, they come ashore only to nest and to raise their young. They are known to ornithologists as "pelagic" meaning simply that they inhabit the open sea. When one considers that the oceans cover some three quarters of the earth's surface, it is remarkable that there are only about 260, or three per cent, of the world's roughly 8,900 or so bird species that may reasonably be called pelagic. These may be divided into 17 groups consisting of the phalaropes, skuas, gulls, terns, penguins, loons, grebes, albatrosses, petrels, shearwaters, storm-petrels, diving-petrels, tropic-birds, gannets, boobies and auks. Not all of the members of these groups of birds live at sea. Some gull species, for example, never reach it. Again, some individuals of some species may live at sea for long periods, while others remain permanently on land. The Herring Gull provides such an example, for some feed all year in fields, while others are found along the shores and in harbors.

It is not unreasonable to argue that members of some other families should be considered pelagic: species seen near the shore that feed, perhaps exclusively, in salt water, for instance. These would include the cormorants, pelicans and frigatebirds. Most of these, although they may feed in the oceans, rest for part of each day on land. A stronger case for inclusion might be made for the various species of marine ducks, such as the scoters, eiders, some mergansers, harlequins and scaup, but most of these feed by diving to the bottom for crustacea, and could not survive in deep water. In *Seabirds* we shall concentrate on those species which are truly birds of the ocean. We shall consider the environment in which they live, and the conditions that make it livable.

To the casual observer the oceans appear to be more-or-less uniform, but this appearance belies an extraordinary diversity of conditions, many of which affect food production. The principal ocean currents are fairly consistent in their patterns, as they are influenced by roughly constant factors: the earth's spin, prevailing winds, the shape of the ocean floor and the coasts. At the same time, these currents are hugely complex. The Atlantic Gulf Stream, for example, delivers an incredible six and a half million cubic yards of warm water per second to the north. When this warm water cools on its northward migration, much of it sinks, and is returned southward at great depth. A similar phenomenon occurs in the Pacific. Where the currents crash together, and along their edges, areas of great turbulence are created. Here, food is most plentiful, not only for birds, but also for the fish and squid on which they feed.

The ocean food chain starts with phytoplankton, a form of plant life a tiny fraction of an inch in diameter, which receives its sustenance from the light of the sun. The chain moves upward through zooplankton to the higher forms of life, the fishes and squids, which in turn feed birds and mammals such as seals. During the brief arctic and antarctic summers, the cold waters near the poles produce prodigious amounts of food at all levels. Krill, tiny, shrimp-like crustaceans, may, under favorable conditions, multiply to some 30,000 to the cubic yard. The water bearing this food is carried into the oceans. It is where these currents, rich with phytoplankton and the animals which eat them, swell to the surface that huge numbers of ocean birds congregate. Mid-ocean areas are generally unfavorable for food production: only about one-third of the Pacific, and half the Atlantic are productive. While this is generally the case, however, the oceans are not homogeneous. Local, relatively small upwellings may be caused by seabed formations and changes in salinity and temperature. In such regions, seabirds thrive. Tropical oceans have the lowest level of food production, which explains the relative lack of food, and consequent dearth of seabirds, in the Caribbean and the Indian Ocean. The Mediterranean is notable for its high salinity and low plankton production. Its entire shearwater population, small in summer, migrates into the Atlantic for the winter.

Seabirds live virtually exclusively on animal matter ranging from zooplankton to fish. The various species of seabirds' bodies have adapted over millions of years, both to their methods of feeding and to their manner of nesting. Generally, bodies are light and small in relation to wing size. This gives many species the ability to glide and, consequently, to cover long distances without undue use of energy. Some species, having adapted to dive from the surface, with their legs far back on their bodies, find it difficult or impossible to walk on land. This limits their choice of nesting sites to ledges, cliffs or trees, from which they can launch themselves into flight.

Feeding methods vary. Tropicbirds, gannets and boobies are plunge-divers; that is, they dive into the water from varying heights to capture their prey in their bills. Among the most spectacular of the plunge-divers is the gannet, which usually folds back its wings about thirty feet above the surface, and so hits the water like a stone. Often, several gannets dive together. Their communal attack appears to keep the fish off-balance, giving them little chance to escape.

Birds such as albatrosses and some shearwaters feed principally while swimming on the surface, although both do plunge-dive on occasion. Surface-taken food ranges from plankton for the smaller petrels, to fish and jellyfish for the albatross. The food may be captured while the birds swim or be plucked from the surface while they're flying.

The tiny and agile storm-petrels feed while on the wing. Some, like Wilson's Storm-petrel, flutter with their legs dangling and feet dappling the surface, making it appear as if they're walking on water. In this way they take plankton and minute larvae. Unlike many other species, which may feed on one or a few large fish, and then rest, petrels feed incessantly throughout the day.

Penguins of all sizes have adapted to swimming under water. They use their wings, useless for flight, for propulsion. Most dive to modest depths in search of krill. Cormorants, loons, and some ducks also feed by swimming below the surface.

Finally, many seabirds are scavengers. Since whaling began, and since fish-processing plants have become seaborne, vast amounts of edible waste have been dumped into the oceans, attracting gulls, albatrosses, fulmars, gannets and other species. This has undoubtedly changed the feeding habits of many individual birds. It is also a boon to first-year immatures, which might not otherwise survive their first winter.

All birds must, of course, come to land to nest, lay their eggs and rear their young. While some species such as loons, phalaropes, gulls, terns and ducks nest inland on ponds, lakes and marshes, the great majority of seabirds find their homes at the edge of the sea, on ledges or cliff tops, or in burrows dug into the earth or sand. Most nest in large colonies, in some of which birds may number in the hundreds of thousands.

In the western Atlantic, there are vast numbers of small islands from Maine to Greenland and Iceland, which provide suitable nesting sites. In Europe, the coasts of Norway, Great Britain and Russia provide many satisfactory cliffs, mostly on rugged islands. Islands tend to provide safety from animal predators.

To attract a large colony cliffs must be high, perhaps 1,500 feet high. They must have ledges for the parent birds to land on, and to raise their young. Every colony houses more than one species. Each species chooses its niche from the spray line to the flat or sloping land at the top of the cliff. Cormorants usually fill the lower tiers. Guillemots, or murres as most are known in North America, make their homes on the sloping ledges of the face. Fulmars nest under overhangs. Gannets occupy the crest of the cliff with gulls and shearwaters and, behind them, the burrow-nesting species such as puffins and storm-petrels. Competition for space between species is not usually a major problem. Only the gannets and fulmars, being more aggressive, often topple the eggs of other species into the sea.

Human interference was probably more of a problem in the nineteenth century than it is today, for egg-taking was then prevalent and affected those bird-colonies situated close to people. Many major sites are now protected as parks or sanctuaries. The size of colonies differs markedly, according to the availability of cliff space, and a reliable food supply within a reasonable flying distance. One colony of Rock-hopper Penguins in the Falkland Islands has some two and a half million pairs. A colony of Chinstrap Penguins in the South Sandwich Islands has 10 million.

Some seabird species have populations in the scores of millions, while others (particularly those which nest on only one remote island) may be limited to a relatively few birds. Accurate counting is never possible. Even aerial photographs of nesting sites cannot reveal the number of birds away from the colony or in their burrows. Nonetheless, competent observers are able to estimate roughly the populations of the various colonies. Several species, including the Short-tailed Alba-tross and the Abbott's Booby have fewer than 5,000 birds. The Cahow or Bermuda Petrel and the Magenta Petrel which were, until recently, thought to be extinct, are down to a few birds. A large number of species have modest populations of between 100,000 and 500,000.

Populations of several gull species are exploding dramatically in many parts of the world. In Great Britain, for instance, Herring Gulls are increasing at a rate of about 13 per cent, per annum. The Ring-billed Gull reappeared in the Great Lakes in 1926, after many years' absence, and has now virtually taken over the waterfront and agricul-tural land around Toronto, Canada. Gulls, which will eat almost anything, are a nuisance in urban areas on both sides of the Atlantic.

The Atlantic populations of murres, razorbills and puffins have declined seriously during the twentieth century. Despite increasing protection from predation by man, most of the decline has occurred since 1960. While the reasons are not entirely clear, oil pollution is certainly one cause. It is likely, however, that a more serious factor is the changing nature of the oceans caused by other forms of chemical and waste pollution, and the consequent effect on the food chain.

Determining the ages to which birds live is difficult. We know, however, that songbirds are relatively short-lived, both on average, and in terms of their maximum expected lifespan. It is likely that only a small percentage of warblers, vireos and flycatchers survive beyond their second year. Since they are capable of breeding after one year, and since they lay from four to eight eggs per clutch, a stable population can still be maintained. Among larger birds such as crows, of which about one half die in their first year, survival beyond 10 years is unusual. By these standards seabirds live a long time — some have been known to survive for more than 50 years.

Scientists studying the longevity of birds rely principally on banding, or ringing, with color-coded leg bands, or marking the birds with dyes. The term "banding" is used in North America; "ringing" is used in Europe. Rings recovered from dead birds tell two things: the time elapsed since ringing, and the place of recovery in relation to the place of ringing. Rings on birds captured alive, often several times, are more informative. The color markings provide continuous data. Seabirds return year after year to their natal colonies where ongoing scientific programs can monitor them. Observation of a large number of color-coded birds, over a reasonable period, allows the calculation of the average mortality rate of birds in varying age brackets and, at the same time, the calculation of average life expectancy. This kind of work is expensive. Relatively inadequate funding by governments and universities has meant that only general conclusions can be drawn, and that data has been taken from only a few of the thousands of active nesting sites.

Birds of all kinds are subject to high mortality in their first year. For many species this is compensated for by large clutches of eggs. Most seabirds, however, lay only one egg and, of those that lay two, it is normal for only one young to survive the nesting period. Many eggs are broken at the nesting site. Many young birds are killed by predators before they reach the water. Cliff nesters often die when they fall. When they reach the water, the young must develop skills to survive starvation, predators and humans. First year mortality for gannets is 75 per cent; for the Wandering Albatross, 70 per cent; and for the Adelie Penguin, 50 per cent. It has been estimated that only 10 per cent of gannets survive to breeding age.

The mortality rate improves as the birds mature, but all are subject to decimation by periodic catastrophes. Starvation is probably the chief threat, followed by storms at sea and accidents. Large birds can survive for long periods without food. They may lose up to 50 per cent of their weight by living on their accumulated fat. When this is gone, however, their digestive systems do not function properly, and they become less and less capable of capturing food, even if it becomes available. Plankton-feeding species, such as the smaller auks, are seriously affected by prolonged storms during which the plankton will not rise to the surface. Starvation usually occurs *en masse*, with changes in current and water temperature. The most notoriously unstable region is off the coast of Peru, where the warm waters are cooled by a prodigious upwelling of cold water. In this area live vast shoals of anchovies, on which both seabirds and fishermen depend for their livelihood. Periodically the current swings far out to sea, warming the water in a phenomenon known as *el niño*. The anchovies descend beyond the birds' capacity to reach them and the birds starve. It has been estimated that the population of these guano birds, pelicans, cormorants and boobies, then falls from about 20 million to as low as one million.

Accidents sometimes occur, mostly at or around nesting sites. Long-winged birds like the albatross, while wonderfully adapted for prolonged gliding, are in danger each time they approach their nesting sites, especially if situated on the faces of cliffs. Terns, which often fly in compact groups while searching for fish, sometimes collide with one another, dislocating or breaking wings. Fishermen inadvertently kill huge numbers of birds in their nets. It is estimated that some 20,000 auks become entangled and die each year in Galway Bay, in Ireland, while drift nets off Greenland account for some half million murres.

While it is impossible to know how long the oldest birds of each species live, there are a number of reliable records for individual birds, which suggest that seabirds are long-lived. There is an authenticated record of a Laysan Albatross surviving in the wild for 53 years. Other known, long-lived seabirds include a Royal Albatross of 46; a Herring Gull, 31; a Caspian Tern, 26; a Manx Shearwater, 23; and a Fairy Tern, 7. The oldest birds probably live much longer, but most birds die younger.

With a low birth rate, high first-year mortality, and the various dangers already mentioned, populations would soon die out if seabirds did not have a long life expectancy. The Great Auk, which was flightless, was hunted to extinction, and the Passenger Pigeon, once the most numerous bird in North America, died out because of habitat destruction during the nineteenth century.

The Red-necked or Northern Phalarope (*Phalaropus lobatus*)   This is a female
in breeding plumage. Its feather pattern is brighter and more distinct than
that of the male.

PHALAROPES

Wilson's Phalarope (*Phalaropus tricolor*)   Male phalaropes incubate the eggs and care for the young in a reversal of the usual gender roles among birds. The nest is a hollow lined with grass and feathers.

This is a small family of only three species of interesting and beautiful birds: the Red (or Grey); the Red-necked (or Northern); and the Wilson's Phalarope. Of the three, the Red and Red-necked are truly pelagic while the Wilson's, which nests in the plains of southern Canada and the northern United States, is terrestrial and winters in South America.

Phalaropes differ from almost all other birds in that the sex roles are reversed. In almost all species, the plumage of the sexes is either similar during the breeding season, or the male is the gaudier of the pair. The female usually incubates the eggs alone or shares this duty with its mate. Upon hatching, the young are fed by the female, either alone or with the male's assistance. All this is reversed in the case of phalaropes. The male phalarope has rather dull markings, and he alone incubates and feeds the young. Within a few days of laying, the female sometimes finds another male in the same area, mates and lays a second clutch of eggs. Pair bonding is, therefore, sometimes brief. It may last only for the few days it takes to complete the clutch, and is unlikely to be renewed.

The two pelagic species with which we are concerned are circumpolar. They arrive in their far northern breeding areas in late May and early June. The female is dominant in choosing a nesting site, and takes command of the display and sexual rituals. Together, they scrape a nest in the tundra, close to water. When the eggs are hatched the young are fully formed. They are capable of leaving the nest for the water within a few hours, and are independent after two weeks. During the period of dependency, the male bird is solicitous in his care of the young, brooding them at night and when the weather is harsh. By late July, the southern migration starts. By August, vast flocks disperse gradually throughout the oceans. The stock from arctic America moves south and east, and by August, flocks in the millions are seen off Maine and Nova Scotia. As the weather hardens, they drift further south across the Atlantic to the coast of Africa. Some fly as far as the Cape of Good Hope. Birds nesting in northern Europe migrate to the Pacific, crossing to the South American coast, some as far south as Chile. The dispersal is truly remarkable: wintering birds inhabit the Indian Ocean, the South China Sea and the Arabian Gulf.

The two pelagic phalaropes, the Red and the Red-necked, are only six to nine inches in length. They are not strong fliers, and they are so buoyant and light that, during storms, they are often blown out of the water. Huge numbers die during violent storms. At sea they are mainly plankton-feeders. They may, however, include tiny fish and crustaceans in their diet, and have also been known to feed on the parasites which inhabit the backs of whales. On the tundra, feeding is varied to include insect larvae, emerging flies and gnats. These may be taken while the bird is swimming or exploring the mud at the edge of a pond or stream. Phalaropes have developed the habit of spinning and darting about on the water, a process thought to stir the water and bring their prey to the surface.

Phalaropes are colorful and beautiful birds with straight, needle-like bills, longish erect necks and lobed toes. In their breeding plumage they are strongly marked and unmistakable. By late summer the molt has discarded most of the colored feathers and by winter they, like almost all shorebirds, are grey and white.

The breast feathers of phalaropes are much like those of ducks in that they retain air, and are almost impervious to water. As a result, these birds sit cork-like, high in the water. The Red Phalarope, known also as the Grey, has a deep chestnut-colored body during the brief nesting season, but for the rest of the year is predominantly grey. The Red-necked has a strong red streak running up the side of the neck and around the line of the head.

Red-necked Phalarope (*Phalaropus lobatus*)   The male, not the female, sits on
the nest. The clutch is usually four eggs. When the young hatch, they head
for water as soon as their feathers are dry.

Red Phalarope (*Phalaropus fulicarius*) The sexes are similar in appearance, but the female (shown here) is brighter. In winter these birds form large flocks far out at sea where they feed on plankton.

Red Phalarope (*Phalaropus fulicarius*) In winter the Red Phalarope loses its brick-red color. It nests across the North American and European Arctic, and spreads out through the Atlantic and Pacific Oceans in winter.

Right: Red-necked Phalarope (*Phalaropus lobatus*) Only about six to nine inches long at maturity, these birds are not strong fliers. Many die during violent storms at sea.

Red-necked Phalarope (*Phalaropus lobatus*)   This is a female, in full plumage, in its nesting site in Canada's Northwest Territories.

SKUAS

Long-tailed Jaeger (*Stercorarius longicaudus*)   It is only when the Long-tailed Jaeger has matured that one can differentiate it with certainty from the Parasitic Jaeger. Here the streamer tail feathers assure identification.

Skuas are dark brown seabirds closely related to gulls. There are seven species which are divided into two groups: the medium to large-sized Great, Chilean, South Polar and Antarctic Skuas; and the somewhat smaller Pomarine, Arctic and Long-tailed Skuas. The members of the latter group, which are known as jaegers in North America, nest only in the northern Arctic. All are fiercely piratical on the nesting grounds, feeding on the eggs and young of other seabirds, and on lemmings. While at sea they attack other birds, force them to disgorge the contents of their crops, and catch it in the air. They are strong and adept on the wing.

Skuas differ from gulls in that their hooked bills are divided into four plates of which one, on the upper mandible, is soft and fleshy, rather like the cere on hawks. The female is somewhat larger than the male. Skuas' legs are black. Their feet are webbed and terminated with strong claws. Common to all mature skuas is an extension of the two central tail-feathers beyond the rest. In four of the species, these feathers are not always easily visible, but with the Pomarine, Arctic and Long-tailed species, it is quite obvious. In the case of the Long-tailed, the two pointed feathers are nearly as long as the rest of the bird.

On migration, the northern-nesting skuas occasionally travel over land, and can been seen near marshes in North America, Europe and Asia. Although it is rare, they have been seen in Europe as far inland as Switzerland and Austria. Most skuas, however, migrate over water on the way to the more temperate oceans. The routes followed by some are prodigious. One skua, ringed in Antarctica, was shot in a Greenland fjord five months later, which established the record for the longest flight determined by ringing.

Skuas are, for the most part, birds of the open oceans. Only the Chilean, which nests along the coast of southern South America, stays relatively close to shore. The Antarctic Skua, which nests on islands in all the southern seas, remains south of the Equator. The South Polar Skua, which nests on the shore of Antarctica, ranges as far north as Alaska. The Great Skua is unique among seabirds in that it nests in both Iceland and Antarctica.

Skuas generally mate for life. Normally, two eggs are laid per clutch and, if food is adequate, both young survive. If food is in short supply, the stronger bird often kills the other. One is always stronger than the other, for the eggs hatch about three days apart.

Skua (*Catharacta skua*)   This is an immature bird on its nest in the Falkland Islands.

Left: Long-tailed Jaeger (*Stercorarius longicaudus*)   This small jaeger weighs less than one pound and has a graceful, bouncy flight. In its nesting ground in the high Arctic it feeds almost exclusively on lemmings.

Pomarine Jaeger (*Stercorarius pomarinus*)   This jaeger bears a superficial resemblance to the much smaller and thinner Parasitic Jaeger. Its elongated tail feathers are, however, spoon-shaped and not pointed.

Parasitic Jaeger (*Stercorarius parasiticus*) Immature jaegers migrate from their circumpolar nesting grounds to all of the oceans. Many immatures remain in the wintering areas for two years before returning north.

Parasitic Jaeger (*Stercorarius parasiticus*)   On their nesting grounds
jaegers feed on lemmings, small birds, shore birds and young ducks. They
carry their prey in their bills and often swallow small birds whole.

GULLS, TERNS & NODDIES

Left: South Polar Skua (*Catharacta lonnbergi*)   Most skuas are truly birds of the ocean. The South Polar Skua nests on the shores of Antarctica but ranges as far north as Alaska.

Ivory Gull (*Pagophila eburnea*)   At maturity, the Ivory Gull is pure white with black legs. Its bill has a reddish tip. Immature birds have faint black dots on their tails and wing feathers, and dark faces.

There are 87 or 88 species of birds in the family *Laridae*, composed of 46 gulls, 38 terns and three or four noddies. Uncertainty as to the precise number arises because of disagreement about the status of one or two species. It is not even certain that gulls, terns and noddies are members of the same family; some authorities hold that they are not.

Gulls, improperly called seagulls by many, originated in the Northern Hemisphere, and have colonized almost every part of the world. The ability of gulls to adapt to different environments is remarkable. The dark Lava or Dusky Gull, of which there are fewer than 1,000 birds, all living in the Galapagos, remains on or close to the shore; the bird seldom alights on the water. The Grey Gull nests in the interior of Peru, and flies to the Pacific to feed. There, it follows trawlers or runs about the shore as the breakers retreat, picking up food.

Most gulls do nest and feed, at least in part, close to the water, either fresh or salt. Inland gull populations in many parts of the world, particularly North America, have been exploding in recent years. We now take large numbers of gulls for granted and, in many urban areas, they have become a nuisance. This present phenomenon is, in a sense, misleading for there have been huge variations in population during the past 200 years. During the seventeenth and eighteenth centuries, gulls were notable items on the tables of the great houses of England and Europe. Huge numbers of birds were taken for food. Early settlers in North America brought with them the taste, not only for gulls' flesh, but also for their eggs. Egging expeditions were carefully organized. Groups of people would visit nesting islands early in the season and smash every egg in a colony. They would return a few days later to collect all the newly-laid eggs, safe in the knowledge that all were fresh. Although the birds would lay again, the mortality rate among the young born late in the season was much higher. In Europe gulls' eggs are available in shops and restaurants, and are very good. Before I knew better, I collected them by the dozen on the marshes in southern England. I would test each egg in warm water: if it floated, it was too old to eat, and was returned immediately to the nest.

Fashion at the end of the nineteenth century demanded, not only feathers, but whole birds on ladies' hats. Gulls and many other species ended up on peoples' heads. Many designers favored long-billed birds, such as waders. Even herons and egrets were a part of this bizarre fad. Frank M. Chapman, of the American Museum of Natural History, made a survey of 700 hats while walking in New York City in 1896. Some 542 were decorated with feathers or whole birds representing, in all, some 40 species. The pressures created by human depredations, whether for food or the millinery trade, became too much for gull colonies along the American seaboard and in many parts of Europe. Many were abandoned. During the 1870s, an ornithologist reported that he did not see one Herring Gull in Rhode Island in four years.

During the 1880s the newly-formed American Ornithologists' Union attempted to have protective legislation introduced. By 1886, Massachusetts had passed a statute imposing a fine of ten dollars for killing, or taking the eggs of, gulls and terns. Although such laws were often ignored, gull populations had begun to rise by the end of the century. In support of the newly-formed AOU Charles Warner, editor and essayist wrote, "A dead bird does not help the appearance of an ugly woman, and a pretty woman needs no such adornment."

Bird populations have, of course, recovered. Man and his garbage have tended to enhance gull populations everywhere.

Of the large gull family, only the two kittiwake species, and the Ross' and Sabine's Gulls can be considered to be truly pelagic. Most gulls are opportunistic. Some gulls, following ships for handouts, may spend weeks in mid-ocean; others feed on golf courses a thousand miles inland.

Terns are generally smaller than gulls. They have longer tails, often forked, and somewhat longer bills. The three skimmer species, which look like terns but are of another family, have a greatly extended lower mandible which cuts the surface of the water as they fly. Terns usually take their food over water. They fly at a modest height, and then plunge-dive when they see prey below the surface. Terns are generally much more pelagic than gulls. Some, such as the Arctic Tern, undertake a fantastic migration of 12,000 miles from the Arctic to Antarctic by both the Atlantic and the Pacific oceans. Others such as the Indian River Tern, the Black-billed Tern, and the Large-billed Tern seldom go to sea.

Terns range in size from the Caspian, with a wingspan of 50 inches, to the Little Tern, with a wingspan of about 20 inches. Nesting habits vary widely. Some use the bare branch of a tree. Others nest in bushes, and some nest on floating vegetation. Species which nest inland often take their prey of insects and other living matter where they can find it. Nesting terns are often the victims of predation by gulls, crows, mammals, and by other large birds. In some tropical areas, Frigatebirds will move through a colony of terns, and feed until satiated on the helpless chicks. Beach-nesting species are subject to so much disturbance of many kinds that they have disappeared as breeding birds from large areas on both sides of the Atlantic.

The three or four species of noddy tern are attractive, dark birds, with black legs and bills. They are not plunge-divers, like most of the other terns, but hover just above the surface in large flocks, and take small prey close to the surface. They are more pelagic than many other terns. They have the capacity to store food which can be regurgitated to feed the young. Noddies are birds of the tropical oceans. In North America, they can best be seen near and beyond the tip of the Florida Keys.

Herring Gull (*Larus argentatus*)   This gull is the common scavenger of the Northern Hemisphere. It is found in coastal areas and inland, eating everything from garbage to fish.

Common Gull (*Larus canus*)   The Common or Mew Gull is primarily Eurasian, but has colonized the western part of North America. It nests for the most part on the edges of ponds and marshes but occasionally, as shown here, in trees.

Fairy Tern (*Sterna nereis*)   In breeding plumage, birds of this species have a black crown and a red bill. They make no nest, but lay and incubate their single egg on the bare branches of trees.

Right: Black-legged Kittiwake (*Larus tridactyla*)   The young bird huddles against the cliff until it is fledged and then launches itself towards the sea.

Left: Bridled Tern (*Sterna anaetheta*)   A seabird primarily, but not exclusively, of the Southern Hemisphere, the Bridled Tern may be seen from Australia and the Malay Archipelago to Africa and the West Indies.

Laughing Gull (*Larus atricilla*)   This black-headed dark-winged gull nests on the eastern seaboard of North America and around the Caribbean, and winters south to Peru.

41

Left: Sabine's Gull (*Larus sabini*) Sabine's Gull nests on marshy ponds in the high Arctic. It lays three eggs in a damp hollow. Vast numbers migrate south as far as Chile and South Africa.

Ring-billed Gull (*Larus delawarensis*) This is the gull commonly seen in North American parks and urban areas. Many do not migrate, but some winter in the Caribbean.

White-capped Noddy
(*Anous minutus*)   Of
the four noddy species
this is the darkest and
has the palest cap. It is
also less pelagic, for
most birds appear to
return to shore at
night, where they roost
in trees and bushes.

Black-legged Kittiwake
(*Larus tridactyla*)
Typically, these ocean-going gulls nest close together on the sloping ledges of high cliffs. The colonies often include other species, such as auks, gannets, murres and puffins.

Brown or Common Noddy (*Anous stolidus*)   These gulls nest on tropical and sub-tropical islands in the Atlantic, Pacific and Indian Oceans. During storms at sea these birds are sometimes driven far beyond their normal ranges.

Glaucous-winged Gull (*Larus glaucescens*)   This large gull has a wingspan of about 54 inches, pale grey wings and a white body. It nests from eastern Russia to British Columbia and drifts south in winter.

Left: Ring-billed Gull (*Larus delawarensis*)   A North American species, the Ring-billed Gull nests in large colonies across Canada and the northern United States.

Black Tern (*Chidonias niger*) The wings of this dainty tern are paler than its body. In flight, it seems almost to dance in the air. It nests in temperate zones in North America and Europe, and migrates to South America and Africa over the winter.

Antarctic Tern (*Sterna vittata*) The Antarctic Tern is similar to the Arctic and South American Terns, and their wide ranges overlap. It nests on islands in the southern oceans from September until May.

Lava Gull (*Larus fuliginosus*)   This gull is found only in the Galapagos
Islands where it scavenges near the fisheries and onshore settlements. It
picks up most of its food along the shoreline and seldom alights on the
water.

Royal Tern (*Sterna maxima*)   This species nests in the Caribbean, western Mexico and the eastern shores of Africa. It tends to wander south from its nesting areas.

Brown or Common Noddy (*Anous stolidus*)   The males and females of this species are alike and their plumage does not vary with the seasons. Young birds are similar to the adult shown here, but lack the pale cap.

Right: Western Gull (*Larus occidentalis*)   The Western gull nests and feeds on the west coast of North America and is seldom seen inland. It is common on beaches and wharves from southern Canada to Mexico.

Franklin's Gull (*Larus pipixcan*)   Breeding in the prairie sloughs of central Canada and the northern United States, the Franklin's Gull winters as far south as the Strait of Magellan. Some go to Western Europe and South Africa.

Swallow-tailed Gull (*Larus furcatus*)   The Swallow-tailed and Sabine's Gulls are similar and their ranges off the coast of South America overlap. Swallow-tailed Gulls nest on the Galapagos Islands. They are unusual in that they normally feed at night, far out at sea.

White-fronted Tern (*Sterna striata*)   This tern breeds in New Zealand and in the surrounding islands but wanders to the coasts of southeastern Australia. It feeds principally in the surf.

Arctic Tern (*Sterna paradisaea*)   The Arctic Tern is similar to the
Common Tern. However, the Arctic Tern is generally paler, and has a longer
tail which extends beyond its wings.

Caspian Tern (*Sterna caspia*)   This large tern with its prominent red bill is almost cosmopolitan in its distribution. It is seen as far south as Australia, and as far north as arctic North America and Scandinavia. It winters inland and in coastal waters.

Right: Least Tern (*Sterna albifrons*)   Perhaps the smallest of terns, the Least or Little Tern has a wingspan of about 20 inches.

Caspian Tern (*Sterna caspia*)   Even this unfledged juvenile possesses the
large bill of the species. The nest is sometimes made in floating vegetation
and sometimes on the ground.

Royal Tern (*Sterna maxima*)   These large terns have a wingspan of about 44 inches. The crests of breeding adult birds are ragged and black to the base of the bill. The ones in the photograph have molted to a ruff at the back of the head.

Herring Gulls (*Larus argentatus*) and Black-backed Gulls (*Larus marinus*) Both
of these species of gull are fiercely predatory.

PENGUINS

Adelie Penguin (*Pigoscelis adeliae*) This is a portion of an Adelie Penguin colony on Hope Bay, Antarctica. Many of the young are lost to predators and many die of starvation before they are capable of fishing for themselves.

There are 18 species of penguin, all flightless, all breeding and feeding in the Southern Hemisphere.

Penguins range in size from the Emperor, which stands about 42 inches high and weighs up to 100 pounds, to the Little Blue (Fairy) of Australia, which is only 16 inches high and weighs about three pounds. Penguins carry a thick layer of blubber and have modified feathers. The blubber acts as insulation and is a source of food. During the three to four-week period of molt, penguins are unable to sustain body heat in the water. They are consequently unable to obtain food and lose about half their body weight. Their blubber keeps them alive. Their feathers are narrow, straight and dense, almost like fur, and have the capacity to hold air. Most of the air is lost during deep dives. Penguins preen vigorously after diving, probably to allow air to re-enter the feathers.

The penguin's flippers are wings which have evolved over time as the bird became more and more aquatic. Similarly, the Galapagos Cormorant has wings which are now so small that they are useless for flight. The bird had no need to fly until people arrived on the Galapagos with their rats and dogs. The birds' survival is now seriously threatened.

Penguins feed below the surface on krill, which are like shrimp, and on fish. The larger penguins consume about five pounds per day. It has been estimated that the five million Adelie Penguins at one breeding site take some 9,000 tons of food daily. In order to catch their prey, penguins have adapted to deep diving. The Emperor Penguin can dive to depths of eight or nine hundred feet and some penguins may remain submerged for as long as 18 minutes. During the dive the penguin's heartbeat slows to one-fifth of the normal rate, which helps to conserve the supply of oxygen in the blood.

Penguins breed on islands throughout the southern oceans, and on the mainlands of Africa, South America, Australia and Antarctica. All but the King and the Emperor build nests or dig burrows, and all are fiercely territorial. Although the females may lay two or three eggs, generally, only one chick survives.

Away from their breeding areas, penguins travel in flocks. There is a pronounced tendency for immature birds to stay together. They also dive in groups. When travelling through water, some species "porpoise" along, swimming some yards under the surface, then "flying" a short distance on their momentum. They may travel at a rate of five or six miles per hour. Penguins tend to be nomadic, rather than migratorial. There is no fixed pattern to their wanderings: they simply follow their sources of food.

The nesting grounds of the Emperor Penguin were first observed by a party of three men from Scott's Antarctic expedition of 1912. These three made a mid-winter journey in the dark, which is described by Apsley Cherry Garrard in his gripping book, *The Worst Journey in the World*. Towing toboggans laden with supplies over broken ice, they suffered terrible privation to make the discovery that Emperors come ashore at the beginning of the winter and lay a single egg on the ice. The penguins then incubate the eggs on their feet. They stay on the ice, going without food for weeks, in order to nurture their eggs. In all there are about 50,000 Emperor Penguins.

The Fairy, or Little Blue Penguin, nests in burrows in Australia and New Zealand. These penguins return to their burrows at night after feeding during the day. At dusk they assemble in rafts off the beach, then waddle ashore in small groups. Following well-worn paths through the dunes, they move inland, some as far as half a mile, or more. The young, waiting in the burrows, are excited and hungry, and rush to meet the parent birds.

Humboldt or Peruvian Penguin (*Spheniscus humboldti*)   The Humboldt Penguin is 25 inches long and has a bare band of pink flesh at the base of the bill. It feeds on schools of anchovies and pilchards off the Peruvian coast — often in competition with fishermen.

Right: Yellow-eyed Penguin (*Megadyptes antipodes*)   Some species of penguin wander widely and stay at sea for months. The Yellow-eyed lives on South Island, New Zealand and other islands in the area, and returns to shore at night. It nests singly or in loose colonies.

Overleaf: King Penguin (*Aptenodytes patagonicus*)   The extent of a colony is shown in this photograph. The vast number of parents seeking food puts a strain on the supply of fish and many young do not survive.

Left: Rockhopper Penguin (*Eudyptes chrysocome*)   The Plumes on the head are the dominant feature of the Rockhopper. These penguins have sharp claws with which to grip the rocky surface of the shores they inhabit.

Adelie Penguin (*Pygoscelis adeliae*)   A wounded Adelie is attacked by others. These penguins are often the prey of sharks and seals.

Left: Humboldt or Peruvian Penguin (*Spheniscus humboldti*) The dark spots on the breast mark this as a mature bird; immatures have white breasts and brown heads. This species breeds on the west coast of South America throughout the year.

Adelie Penguins (*Pygoscelis adeliae*)   Each Adelie Penguin takes about five pounds of food per day, mostly krill and small fish. During the molt, they remain on the ice and fast, losing about one quarter of their weight in the process.

Gentoo Penguin (*Pygoscelis papua*)   The distinguishing feature of the adult Gentoo Penguin is the white band from behind the eyes across the back of the head.

Chinstrap Penguin
(*Pygoscelis antarctica*)
One colony of
Chinstrap Penguins in
the South Sandwich
Islands numbers some
10 million birds.
Numbers are believed
to be increasing
because of the
decrease in the
number of whales with
which they compete
for food.

Right: Emperor Penguin
(*Aptenodytes forsteri*)
Largest of the penguin
family, the Emperor
can dive to depths of
more than 800 feet, and
may remain
submerged for up to 18
minutes.

LOONS

Left: King Penguin (*Aptenodytes patagonicus*)   The King Penguin breeds on islands north of Antarctica. It has brightly-colored patches on the chin and neck. It breeds twice every three years and goes ashore between September and March.

Common Loon or Great Northern Diver (*Gavia immer*)   The Common Loon breeds in the northern United States, throughout Canada, and in parts of Greenland and Iceland. It winters as far south as Gibralter and the Caribbean.

The five species of the family *Gaviidae*, known as loons in North America and as divers in Europe, have somewhat different names on the two sides of the Atlantic. They are:

Europe	North America
Red-throated Diver	Red-throated Loon
Black-throated Diver	Arctic Loon
Great Northern Diver	Common Loon
White-billed Diver	Yellow-billed Loon
Pacific Diver	Pacific Loon

The Pacific Loon (to use the North American nomenclature) was, until 1985, considered to be a sub-species of the Arctic Loon, but the American Ornithologist's Union has now recognized it as a fifth species. The Pacific Loon is slightly smaller than the Arctic Loon, has a smaller bill, and minor differences in plumage.

Loons are large birds with a vague resemblance to ducks and cormorants. All loons breed and live in the Northern Hemisphere. They sit low in the water and feed on fish for the most part, although they also take crabs, underwater insects, crayfish, crustaceans, and some vegetable matter. They usually remain submerged for less than a minute, but have been observed at depths of 240 feet. They propel themselves in the water using their large, webbed feet, with an occasional assist from their wings.

In the air, loons are strong, fast fliers, although their wings are relatively small and set far back on their bodies. Because their legs, too, are set well back on their bodies all loons, other than the Red-throated, are unable to stand and walk in an upright position. They must shove themselves along on their breasts. For this reason, they nest on mounds, or in marshes, only a few inches above the water. The combination of small wings and heavy bodies makes it awkward for all, except Red-throated Loons, to become airborne. They launch themselves into the air after a furious run into the wind along the surface of the water. They, again with the exception of the Red-throated, are incapable of taking off from the land. Once in the air, loons are quite easy to spot, for they carry their necks lower than their bodies. This gives them a hunchbacked appearance. The Common, Arctic, and Pacific Loons have straight, conical bills, while the Yellow-billed and Red-throated Loons have bills that are slightly up-turned.

In breeding plumage, all of the loons are strongly-marked, elegant birds, with heavy-looking necks and a sleek appearance. The Common Loon nests from Iceland west to Alaska, while the other species nest in northern Europe as well. All species winter to a large extent in salt water, either along the coast or at sea. Some, however, remain inland, moving south only far enough to find food and open water.

Arctic Loon or Black-throated Diver (*Gavia arctica*)   The breeding range of
the Arctic Loon extends across northern North America, Europe and Asia. It
winters offshore in the Pacific and eastern Atlantic, but is rarely seen in
eastern North America.

Red-throated Loon or Red-throated Diver (*Gavia stellata*) Unlike other loons, the Red-throated is capable of standing upright. It can also take off from the water without a long run on the surface. It lays two dark brown eggs which must be incubated for about 26 days.

Arctic Loon (*Gavia arctica*)   The Arctic Loon almost invariably nests at the edge of a pond or lake. These birds are unable to walk upright and must shove themselves along the ground.

GREBES

Western Grebe (*Aechmophorus occidentalis*) Although grebes bear a superficial resemblance to ducks, they are distinguished by their pointed bills and short tail-feathers. The toes of the grebe have flat lobes and are not webbed.

There are 19 or 20 species of grebe, of which at least one species occurs on all of the principal land masses of the world, with the exception of Antarctica. They all breed on fresh water, most on masses of rotting vegetation found floating in marshes. Some species never reach salt water, while a few, the Red-necked, the Great Crested, the Horned and Black-necked are truly pelagic in winter. Others, such as the Western Grebe of North America and the Great Grebe of southern South America, disperse to coastal waters in winter.

Many of the grebe species are noted for their elaborate and spectacular courtship displays, in which they may run along the surface of the water in an upright position, singly or in pairs. When alarmed they tend to dive rather than fly, usually swimming underwater to the protection of the marsh. They also have the ability, shared with loons, to compress the air from their body feathers, and submerge, so that only their eyes and nostrils remain above the surface. When diving, several species launch themselves upward and forward with their feet, clearing the surface as they do, before disappearing in the manner of some of the smaller ducks.

In appearance grebes bear a superficial resemblance to ducks, especially at a distance, on the water. Many, however, have rather long and slender necks, and all have pointed bills and short tail-feathers. In water, they steer with their feet, which trail behind them when they're flying. The toes of grebes have flat lobes and are not webbed.

Grebes range in size from the nine-inch Least, which is found from Texas to northern Argentina, and which seldom leaves fresh water, to the 24-inch Great Grebe of South America. In breeding plumage, some species have pronounced tufts, crests and facial markings. Like loons, the necks and heads are carried below the line of the back in flight.

Eared or Black-necked Grebe (*Podiceps nigricollis*)   The Eared Grebe nests in marshy regions on all continents except Australia. In winter it loses the gaudy yellow "ears" and becomes a drab grey and white.

Pied-billed Grebe (*Podilymbus podiceps*) The Pied-billed Grebe is rarely seen on salt water. It nests from northern Canada to the tip of South America.

Eared Grebe (*Podiceps nigricollis*)   Like other grebes, the Eared nests on fresh water. It is one of only a few, however, that seeks salt water in its migrations.

Left: Red-necked Grebe (*Podiceps grisegena*)   The Red-necked Grebe is widespread across inland regions in the Northern Hemisphere in summer and disperses to coastal waters in winter.

Western Grebe (*Aechmophorus occidentalis*)   A long-necked dark and white bird with a wingspan of about 40 inches, the Western Grebe nests only in western North America and migrates to coastal waters from Mexico to British Columbia in the winter.

Horned Grebe (*Podiceps auritus*)   The nest is made in a mass of floating vegetation, usually in the open, but anchored to nearby growth. There are usually four eggs, although only two can be seen here.

THE TUBENOSE ORDER
OF BIRDS

Shy or White-capped Albatross (*Diomedea cauta*)   The nesting colony of the Shy Albatross off Tasmania was once huge. Plume hunters had reduced the colony to 250 nests by 1909, but it has since recovered to about 2,000. The Shy Albatross nests off southern Australia and New Zealand and wanders west as far as Africa.

This order of birds is distinguished by tube-like external nostrils on either the top or side of the upper mandible. The bills are formed of lateral plates which are separated by grooves. In all species, the bill is hooked downward at the tip. The order consists of the following families: albatrosses (13 species); petrels and shearwaters (61 species); storm-petrels (21 species); and diving-petrels (four species). They range in size from the Wandering Albatross, which is the world's largest seabird, with a wingspan of up to nearly 12 feet, to the Least Storm-petrel which is only six inches long, and has a wingspan of 12 inches. Tubenoses are truly pelagic birds, in that they spend all of their lives at sea, except during the breeding period.

All tubenoses have the ability to convert their food into an oily mass which, stored in their stomachs, can be regurgitated directly into the stomachs of their chicks. Up to four pounds can be transferred at a time by the largest albatrosses. This faculty permits the parent birds to be away from their young for some days on feeding trips.

Albatrosses

The albatrosses are the largest of the tubenoses. They have long, slender wings on which they soar close to the water, rising into the wind, then sailing down, always searching for food. They are long-lived birds with an average life expectancy of something under 30 years. Almost all are colonial nesters. The inhabitants of their colonies may number in the thousands. They nest on mounds, or in hollows scooped out of windswept slopes, on terraces or on flat ground. One of the nesting sites of the Laysan Albatross is on Midway Island, in the Pacific. When the US Air Force built a base on Midway, the landing strip was placed right through the breeding area. During World War II and for some time after, aircraft-bird collisions were regular occurrences, for the birds did not abandon the site.

The two species of albatross, the Wandering and the Royal, which do not breed until their ninth or tenth year, have long periods of incubation and care of the young: about 11 months. Consequently they nest only every second year. The other species nest annually.

All albatrosses feed principally on the surface, mostly on squid, although they are also capable of submerging. They are vulnerable to predation by sharks and other large fish; indeed, one shark was found to have the bodies of 13 albatrosses in its stomach, and the feathers of several more. Most species of albatross nest and range through the southern oceans, although three, the Short-tailed, the Black-footed and the Laysan, wander as far north in the Pacific as Alaska and Siberia. One, the Chatham Island Albatross, remains close to the island which gives it its name, east of New Zealand.

Petrels & Shearwaters

The family of petrels and shearwaters includes the fulmar-petrels (or giant petrels), the fulmars, the shearwaters, the prions, the petrels and the gadfly-petrels. In all there are 72 species. They differ in structure from the albatrosses in that their nostrils are united in one tube. Most feed exclusively at sea. The shearwaters are the principal followers of ships at sea; near land they are joined in this pursuit by gulls. Although they do feed on refuse thrown over the sides of ships, it is likely that they are most interested in the squid and shrimp pushed to the surface by the ships' wakes. Many species of this family nest in colonies or burrow in soft soil or sand.

We once sat for hours on a beach on Philip Island in south Australia watching Short-tailed Shearwaters flying back and forth over the water. At dusk they came close to the shore and, just at dark, flew in hundreds to their burrows in the dunes behind us.

At sea, most birds seen at a distance are difficult to identify. They usually appear to be uniformly dark. It is also difficult to determine the size of one in relation to another. The fact that each species goes through a number of distinct and intermediate color phases before reaching maturity increases the confusion. The Giant Petrel, for instance, closely resembles some of the albatrosses, although the latter have longer bills. The fulmars look like gulls. Thus, this family presents great problems for the few who can observe them in flight, be they off-shore fishermen, ocean travellers or those who go on pelagic tours. Relatively few people are able to visit remote island nesting sites where identification is simpler. In a general way, it is fair to say that the members of the shearwater family have long slender wings and relatively short bodies.

Storm-petrels

There are some 23 species of storm-petrel living in both hemispheres. Individual species are notoriously difficult to identify, but as a group they are smaller than other petrels and shearwaters, and most appear to be black from a distance. Most species have white rumps and some are white on the underside of the wings. Those breeding in the Northern Hemisphere have somewhat more pointed wings than those in the south — not a very reliable identification guide.

Some species tend to stay close to their nesting grounds. Others, such as the Wilson's Storm-petrel, migrate from Antarctica, north as far as Greenland, and throughout the Indian and Pacific Oceans. It is probably the world's most abundant seabird.

Storm-petrels feed while flying, fluttering just above the surface with their feet dangling. Since they do not gorge on a single capture, but feed on larvae and plankton, they must feed all day. They range in size from five inches to about 10 inches in length.

Diving-petrels

There are four species of diving-petrels; all reside in the Southern Hemisphere. They are auk-like little birds, with short wings on which they buzz over the ocean with furious energy. They often fly into a steep wave, in the manner of some auks, emerging from the other side, still flying.

This small group differs from other petrels in that it has two tube-like nostrils instead of one. These birds are not great wanderers.

Wedge-tailed Shearwater (*Puffinus pacificus*)   The Wedge-tailed Shearwater
nests widely throughout the central Pacific and in the Indian Ocean. The
shape of the tail is not a reliable guide in identification.

Waved Albatross (*Diomedea irrorata*)   Other albatrosses soar easily but the Waved is not as adept. It must flap frequently, even in a strong breeze. It nests in the Galapagos Islands and wanders to the coasts of Peru and Equador.

Wedge-tailed Shearwater (*Puffinus pacificus*) The Wedge-tailed Shearwater, shown here in its dark phase, feeds exclusively at sea. It makes its nest in sandy burrows on island beaches or mainland shores.

Giant Fulmar or Giant Petrel (*Macronectes giganteus*)   The external tube through which the members of this family breathe is visible on the upper mandible. The bills of all of the tubenoses are hooked at the tip and divided in plates.

Greater Shearwater (*Puffinus gravis*)   The remote southern Atlantic islands,
Nightingale, Inaccessible, Tristan da Cunha and Gough are the breeding
grounds of the Greater Shearwater. Numbers have increased from about two
to four million in this century.

Wandering Albatross (*Diomedea exulans*) Like most other albatrosses, the Wandering Albatross is a bird of the southern oceans. It has no fixed migratory pattern.

Giant Fulmar (*Macronectes giganteus*) Fulmars are closely related to the albatrosses, but do not have their grace or ability to glide. Fulmars lumber along with heavy wingbeats and short glides.

Left: Black-browed Albatross (*Diomedea melanophris*) Albatrosses are colonial nesters — some colonies number about 10,000 birds. They often mix with the Grey-headed Albatross in the nesting area. The egg is incubated for about 68 days.

Fork-tailed Storm-petrel (*Oceanodroma furcata*). This species is
northern Pacific Ocean and nests from British Columbia to
Alaskan population is estimated to be about five million.

Great Skua (*Catharacta skua*)   During the nesting season birds display to
attract a mate. When at sea, birds of this species tend to be solitary. They
occasionally follow ships for scraps, or for food churned up in their wakes.

Leach's Storm-petrel (*Oceanodroma leucorhoa*). Leach's Storm-petrel
on shores throughout the Northern Hemisphere. It is only about
and has an 18-inch wingspan. Its flight is buoyant, and often near
the surface of the ocean while in search of food.

Light-mantled Albatross (*Phoebetria palpebrata*)   The southern oceans are the nesting and feeding grounds of this albatross. It returns to its colonies in September or October; its young are fledged and away in the following April or May.

Black-browed Albatross (*Diomedea melanophris*). With its eight-foot wingspan, the albatross can soar while using a minimum of energy. It feeds mostly at night, dipping to the surface of the ocean. It can store food in its stomach, to be regurgitated later directly into the stomach of its young.

THE PELICAN ORDER
OF BIRDS

Blue-footed Booby (*Sula nebouxii*)   The streaked, heavily-feathered neck is typical of this species. The booby nests throughout the year. Its feeding range varies according to the availibility of fish and fluctuations in the currents of the sea.

The order of p...
and ...oobies
darters (two...
(three species). All...
otherwise come in...
less pelagic than th...
and darters are res...
tropicbirds and boo...
order nest on the g...
order is capable of...
of the boobies, dart...
in mangroves.

Tropicbirds
The three species of...
the most spectacul...
black in the second...
with equally long o...
and fan-shaped tails...

These birds are...
but can sometimes...
they do not appear...
see them at any tim...
in loose colonies. H...
lay their eggs.

At sea they fl...
they fold their wings...
When they emerge th...
are protected from...
the skin of the b...
occasionally associa...

Both the Red-t...
Atlantic and Caribb...
The Red-tailed only...

Gannets & Boobies
The nine species of...
are all large; posse...
wedge-shaped tails...
of the Atlantic, the G...

Gannet, all have white bodies and wings with black tips, pale bills and a golden wash at the back of the head. They differ only in the tips of the tails. During the winter, the Northern Gannet moves south, along the shores of North America and Europe, and into the Atlantic where it can often be seen from the shore. Gannets are rather more pelagic than the darker boobies which, although quite capable of resting in the water, tend to come ashore at night.

Boobies are sometimes confused with one another, and with immature gannets. Only the Blue-faced and the Red-footed Boobies stand out: the coloration of their legs and feet is conclusive.

The members of this group are direct fliers who use an alternating flapping and soaring pattern of flight. All are plunge-divers, falling on their prey from heights of up to 100 feet. Gannets dive vertically, boobies at an angle.

The gannets nest at the tops of cliffs, on sloping or flat ground, seldom more than 25 yards from the edge. There is a colony on Bonaventure Island at the tip of the Gaspé Peninsula in the Atlantic Ocean. Here there is the usual progression up the face of the cliff: kittiwakes, murres and auks, and finally, gannets. Guardrails have been placed only a few yards from the nests but the birds appear not to be disturbed by visitors. These nesting cliffs are full of the activity of birds arriving and leaving at all levels. They resound to the quarrelling of birds intent on maintaining their territories, and with the greeting calls of sitting birds.

Left: Northern Gannet (*Sula bassana*)   Gannets generally nest on the sloping ground at the tops of cliffs. Kittiwakes and murres fill the intermediate and lower ledges, as close to the water as the splash line.

White Pelican (*Pelecanus erythrorhynchos*)   Pelicans nest, for the most part, on the ground. They are not so closely associated with the sea as many of the other species to which they are related — gannets, boobies and tropicbirds, for example.

Preceding pages: Northern Gannet (*Sula bassana*)   Some colonies of gannets number about 50,000 birds. The total population of this species is probably in the vicinity of half a million birds.

Blue-footed Booby (*Sula nebouxii*)   This species is found mainly on the coasts of northern South America, and as far north as Mexico. Staying, generally, close to the shore, they dive at an angle into the water to take their prey.

Red-billed Tropicbird (*Phaeton aethereus*)   This tropicbird may nest in caves, on ledges or in stony cavities in the ground. Its egg is laid on bare rock. Nesting may occur at any time of the year; there is no regular migration pattern.

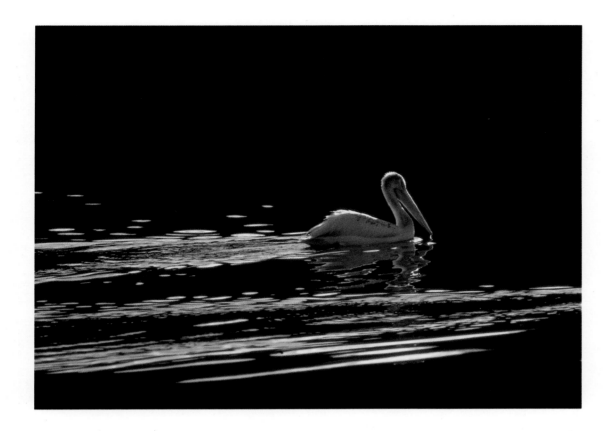

White Pelican (*Pelecanus erythrorhynchos*) Pelican populations are dependent on the supply of food. Sudden changes in currents, like the phenomenon known as *el niño* off Peru, may drastically reduce their number.

Red-billed Tropicbird (*Phaeton aethereus*) The long streamer tail is apparent on this beautiful and agile bird. When not nesting, it wanders about the ocean, flying between 30 and 50 feet above the surface. It takes its prey by plunging into the water.

Right: Northern Gannet (*Sula bassana*) Although the territory of a pair of gannets may be only a foot or so in breadth, it is generally fiercely defended against intrusion. If, however, a chick slides into the nest unnoticed, it will be cared for.

Left: Red-footed Booby (*Sula sula*) Wide spread throughout the tropical oceans, the Red-footed Booby nests only in forested islands, for it builds its nests in trees.

Northern Gannet (*Sula bassana*) About 90 per cent of gannets return to the same nest site, and to the same mate, year after year. It is unlikely, however, that the pair remains together in the winter.

Blue-faced or Masked Booby (*Sula dactylatra*) The Blue-faced Booby feeds principally on flying fish which it captures in dives from about 30 feet above the surface of the ocean.

Right: Blue-faced Booby (*Sula dactylatra*) This bird breeds and travels widely through all of the tropical seas. There are four sub-species of Blue-faced Booby, but the differences in appearance are not readily noticed.

Previous Pages: Northern Gannet (*Sula bassana*) During the day there is constant traffic and noise at a gannet colony. The sitting females welcome the males, and the fish they bring, with loud squawks.

Left: Northern Gannet (*Sula bassana*) During the winter, the Gannet moves south along the shores of North America and Europe, and into the Atlantic where it can often be seen from the shore.

Brown Pelican (*Pelecanus occidentalis*) A wingspan of nearly seven feet is needed to carry this eight-pound bird which glides and flaps as it flies close to the surface of the water. On sighting fish, it rises a few feet then plunges after its prey.

Red-billed Tropicbird (*Phaeton aethereus*)   Although tropicbirds are usually solitary and far at sea, during the nesting season they remain near the shore. This species nests on the Pacific coasts from Mexico to Columbia, the Caribbean, the Atlantic and Indian Oceans.

AUKS

Atlantic Puffin (*Fratercula arctica*)   The Atlantic Puffin nests from
Newfoundland to Britain, through Greenland, Iceland, Scandinavia and the
Russian islands. There are three sub-species, but they are not readily
distinguishable.

There are 22 species of auk. All nest and range through the North Pacific and North Atlantic. In ecological terms they are the counterpart in the Northern Hemisphere of the penguins and diving-petrels. Although all surviving auks can fly (penguins cannot), the two groups bear a superficial resemblance. In color, auks are mostly dark and white, although some have brightly colored bare parts. They float low in the water, have densely-packed breast feathers, and when on land, they sit upright on legs set back on their bodies about as far as they can be. The larger species feed on fish, while the smaller ones live on plankton. The group includes the murres, the Razorbill, puffins, auklets and murrelets.

Of the auks, the puffins are probably the best known. They have absurdly large, multi-colored bills, bright red legs, and webbed feet. Although they are burrow-nesters they do not, like the petrels, come ashore only at night. Puffins can be seen in their nesting colonies during the day as well. When the young are fairly advanced, the parents abandon the burrows and fly far out to sea. When the young become hungry enough, they follow. Mature birds shed their gaudy bills after the nesting season, and grow another. During the winter it is unusual to see puffins near land, for they generally feed in loose flocks in mid-ocean. Here they molt and become flightless for a time. Puffins feed on small fish which they carry to their nests neatly stowed, laterally to the body, alternating fish heads and tails. This arrangement occurs because the puffin, swimming under water through a school of fish, takes one on one side and then the other.

On a typical nesting cliff, the Common Murres lay their eggs on narrow ledges, shoulder to shoulder in tiers, below the kittiwakes. Nesting ledges often slope dangerously downward, but the eggs are shaped to resist rolling.

The seven species of murrelets live only in the Pacific. They remain close to shore and can be seen quite easily with binoculars. Murrelets have varied nesting habits, most being non-colonial. They find holes in trees or near the ground, some miles from the sea.

Auks' bodies carry a lot of fat which has been used by people as bait for fishing. The first bird species to be exterminated by the white man in North America was the Great Auk. This bird had grown too large for its wings and, since it could not fly, became the prey of Atlantic fishermen. Vast numbers of Great Auks were bashed to death with sticks or, where practicable, marched into boats, killed and eaten fresh or salted. For many years ocean fishermen relied so heavily on the auks that they would leave port knowingly under-provisioned. When numbers declined, the fishermen were puzzled. When the last auk was bludgeoned to death, on a small island off Iceland in 1844, they were astonished that there were no more.

Horned Puffin (*Fratercula corniculata*)   This is a mature bird with a fully-developed bill. Note the pink reflection on the belly from the orange feet. Horned Puffins may travel two or three hundred feet above the water.

Atlantic Puffin (*Fratercula arctica*)   This photograph illustrates the hump-backed attitude of the Puffin in flight, especially as it comes in to land. The prominent bill and trailing orange feet are visible from a considerable distance.

Left:
Parakeet Auklet
(*Cyclorrhynchus psittacula*) This species nests in the Aleutian Islands and north to the Bering Strait. It winters in the north Pacific.

Thick-billed Murre (*Uria lomvia*) Thick-billed Murres use every available surface on a cliff to lay their eggs. Their breeding range overlaps that of the Common Murre, but the Thick-billed nests much farther north.

133

Atlantic Puffin (*Fratercula
arctica*)   Puffins winter far out at
sea where they feed on small fish.
They molt towards the end of the
winter and are flightless for a
period before returning to their
nesting areas.

Common Murre or Guillemot (*Uria aalge*) The Common Murre has comparatively short wings. It is heavy in relation to wing size, and must flap fast and hard to remain airborne.

Thick-billed Murre (*Uria lomvia*)   Even at a distance, one can distinguish the
thin white line like a long eyelash which marks some, but not all Thick-
billed Murres.

Common Murre (*Uria aalge*)   Some Murre colonies number in the millions of birds. They range along the shores of North America, Europe and Asia.

Left: Horned Puffin (*Fratercula corniculata*)   The Horned Puffin of the Pacific is similar to, and closely related to, the Atlantic Puffin. After the nesting season the prominent casing on the bill is shed, leaving a smaller, dark one with a red tip.

Parakeet Auklet (*Cyclorrhynchus psittacula*)   The Parakeet Auklet is only about ten inches long. Like most auks, it ranges chiefly on northern shores in the Northern Hemisphere.

Left: Razorbill (*Alca torda*) and Common Murre (*Uria aalge*)   These species are similar in size, stance, and in the shape of the bodies. The blunt bill of the Razorbill and the slim, pointed bill of the Murre make it easy to tell them apart.

Common Murre (*Uria aalge*)   The Murre lays its single egg on the bare edge of a cliff. The egg is shaped and weighted in a manner that helps to keep it from rolling.

Razorbill (*Alca torda*)   This Razorbill nests on cliffs in the North Atlantic. In winter it often joins other species of auks to form enormous "rafts" on the water.

PHOTOGRAPH CREDITS

Index to Photographs